Maïte Roche

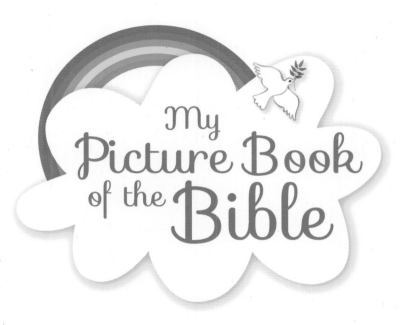

My
Picture Book
of the Bible

MAGNIFICAT · Ignatius

Contents

The New Testament

Creation

The breath of God

Light

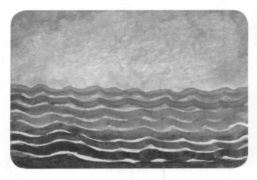

Water and sky

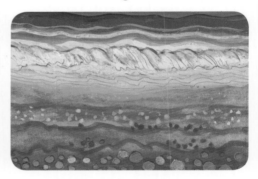

The land and the sea

In the beginning, God created the world. Through his Word, he created the heavens and the earth, and he saw that everything was good. His Spirit is the breath of life.

Plants, flowers, and grains

Trees

Fruit

Day and Night

The sun

The moon and the stars

God created the sun to light up the day, and the moon and the stars to light up the night. They mark the rhythm of time and the four seasons of the year.

Spring

Summer

Autumn

Winter

Fish

God created the fish and other creatures that live in the water.
There are big ones and tiny ones, blue ones, red ones, yellow
ones, green ones, white ones, and black ones.

A fish

A whale

A seahorse

A dolphin

A starfish

An octopus

A crab

Seashells

A turtle

Birds

God created birds with wings to fly in the sky.
They have beautiful feathers in all kinds of colors!

A nest full of eggs

Nestlings

Feeding time

A parrot

A chickadee

A pigeon

A rooster

A hen

Chicks

Animals

God created all the animals, from the smallest to the biggest.
Some live in the forest, and others live in the countryside,
the desert, or the plains.

A lion

A panda

An elephant

A cat

A squirrel

A mouse

A hedgehog

A butterfly

Ants

Man and Woman

God created man and woman. He said to them,
"Multiply and fill the earth. I entrust it to you." God saw that
his creation was very good, and he blessed it. But Adam and Eve
disobeyed God and had to leave the garden of Eden.

The garden

Adam and Eve

The tree

The serpent

Disobedience

Paradise lost

The families of the world

Noah's Ark

It rained for forty days and forty nights. It was the flood!
Noah's ark alone floated on the waters. When the flood was over,
life could start all over again. God said, "The rainbow is
the sign of my covenant of love for ever."

Noah's ark

Noah and his family

The flood

The olive branch

The dove

The rainbow

Two animals of every kind

Abraham

God said to Abraham, "Leave your land and your home. Go to a country that I will show you. You will be the father of a people as numerous as the stars in the sky."

Abraham and Sarah

The departure
for the Promised Land

The caravan of camels and flocks of sheep

A tent

The birth of Isaac

Rebekah

Rebekah gave a drink of water to Abraham's servant
and his ten camels, and she was chosen to be the wife of
Abraham's son Isaac. After they were married, they had twins:
Esau was born first, and then Jacob.

The servant

A jug

A well

Isaac greets his bride-to-be.

The marriage of Isaac and Rebekah

The twins

Esau and Jacob

Esau and Jacob grew up. One day, Esau came home from
the hunt tired and hungry. Jacob said to him, "I will give you this
bowl of stew if you let me take your place as the firstborn."
Esau agreed. Their father, Isaac, later blessed Jacob,
and he became the head of the family.

Esau the hunter

Jacob the shepherd

A bow and arrow

A goat

A gazelle

A rabbit

A bowl of stew

Isaac's blessing

Joseph and His Brothers

Jacob had twelve sons. He gave Joseph a beautiful coat.
His big brothers were very jealous. They sold Joseph to some
merchants who took him to Egypt as a slave. But God protected
Joseph, who became Pharaoh's minister and saved his people.

The coat

Twenty pieces
of silver

Joseph
the prisoner

Pharaoh

Joseph the minister

Joseph forgives his brothers.

Moses Saved from the Waters

The people of God had become slaves in Egypt. One day, Pharaoh's daughter found a little Hebrew baby in a basket. She said to him, "You will be my son, and I will call you Moses because I saved you from the waters."

Pharaoh's daughter

Moses

The pyramids

The enslaved people

A lily pad

A dragonfly

Papyrus plants

God Calls Moses

God spoke from the burning bush. Moses answered, "Here I am!"
God said to him, "Go free my people, who are suffering
in Egypt. You will lead them, and I will help you."
So Moses set off with his family.

The bush

Fire

The burning bush

"Here I am!"

A shepherd's staff

Sandals

The mountain

Moses leaves for Egypt.

Moses and Pharaoh

With his brother Aaron, Moses said to Pharaoh,
"Let my people go." But Pharaoh refused. So God sent terrible
plagues. At last, Pharaoh shouted, "Go!" On the night of their
departure, each family shared a meal in celebration,
for God had freed his people.

Moses and Aaron

Pharaoh

A servant

A scribe

A harpist

An Egyptian priest

The Passover meal

A Path through the Sea

Pharaoh chased after the people of God with his soldiers and charioteers. God opened up a path through the sea, and his people passed through on dry ground. Then the sea closed up again, and Pharaoh's army was destroyed. The people were saved and sang a victory song.

Pharaoh's chariot

Horses and horsemen

Moses stretches out his hand.

The passage through the sea

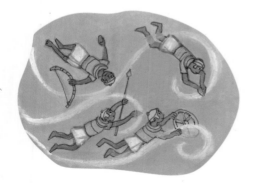

Soldiers thrown into the sea

The song of victory

In the Desert

God took care of his people and gave them bread (manna) and water. "I am your God," he said. "Love me with all your heart." He gave Moses Ten Commandments so that his people could live together in peace. Moses wrote them on stone tablets and placed them in the ark of the covenant.

The desert

Manna

The water from the rock

The tablets of the law

The ark of the covenant

The Promised Land

David, the Shepherd of Bethlehem

Every day, David went out to watch over his flock. He sang to God as he played on the harp, "The Lord is my shepherd; I shall not want." He was the youngest child of the family, but God chose him. He was anointed the future king.

The song of David

A harp

A flock

A ram

A ewe

A lamb

Bethlehem

David's anointing

David Battles Goliath

The giant Goliath shouted loudly, "Come do battle with me. Whoever's the strongest wins the war!" David replied, "It is God who grants victory." With that, he shot a stone with his slingshot at the forehead of the giant, who collapsed and was vanquished.

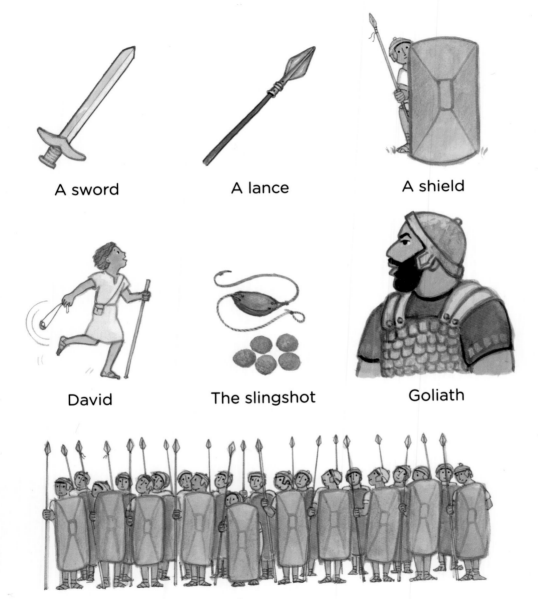

A sword

A lance

A shield

David

The slingshot

Goliath

An army

The Procession to Jerusalem

King David danced in front of the ark of the covenant. It was carried in procession amid shouts of joy, to the sounds of horns and flutes and lyres and cymbals. There was a great celebration to welcome God to Jerusalem.

The procession

A horn

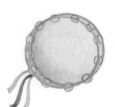

A tambourine

A lyre

Cymbals

The dance of David

A flute

Solomon's Temple

King Solomon, King David's son, had a magnificent Temple
built for the ark of the covenant. He wanted God to have
a beautiful house, so that the people could worship him properly.

The builders

The stones

The columns

The offerings

The altar

A menorah

The prayer of the king

The Temple

The Queen of Sheba

The queen of Sheba arrived with great fanfare to visit King Solomon. She was full of admiration for his wisdom, his palace, and the Temple. She offered him precious gifts and said to him, "Blessed be your God, who made you king!"

The queen

The king

A crown

The procession

The palace

The gifts

The Prophets

Samuel listens to God.

Elijah regains courage.

Isaiah foretells the Savior.

Jeremiah laments.

God called prophets. They listened to his Word and told it
to the people: "A Savior is to come. All peoples
will walk toward his light."

Ezekiel sees a river of living waters flowing from the Temple.

Daniel hopes in God in the midst of the lions.

Jonah spends three days in the belly of a whale.

The Annunciation

"Hail, Mary, full of grace," said the angel Gabriel. "Rejoice,
for God has chosen you to be the mother of Jesus,
the Son of God, the promised Savior." And Mary said,
"Yes, I am the handmaid of the Lord."

The house of Anne and Joachim, Mary's parents

Flowers

The angel Gabriel

Mary

Mary and Elizabeth

Mary and Joseph

The Nativity

Jesus was born in Bethlehem. He was laid in a manger. Alerted by the angels, shepherds came to adore him. Mary and Joseph were filled with wonder. "Glory to God and peace on earth!"

The angels' hymn

The announcement
to the shepherds

The stable

The manger

Mary and Jesus

The donkey

Baby Jesus

The ox

The Three Wise Men

Three wise men saw a new star in the sky: "A new king is born;
let us go worship him!" They traveled a long way following
the star and were filled with joy upon seeing Jesus.
They offered him gifts: gold, frankincense, and myrrh.

Caspar, Balthasar, and Melchior

The star

The adoration of the Magi

Gold, frankincense, and myrrh

Jesus and his mommy

The Presentation of Jesus in the Temple

Joseph and Mary went to the Temple. They made an offering of two turtledoves to thank God for the birth of Jesus. Old Simeon said with great joy, "Here is the Savior, the light of the world!" And Anna sang in praise of God.

The turtledoves

A light

Simeon's joy

Anna the prophetess

The Holy Family

Jesus, Mary, and Joseph lived in a house in Nazareth.
Jesus grew up. He was filled with wisdom
and the love of God, his Father.

The Holy Family

Joseph the carpenter

His tools

Jesus' first steps

Jesus, his grandma, and his mommy

Prayer

Jesus at school

61

Jesus in the Jerusalem Temple

When he was twelve years old, Jesus spoke about God
with the scribes and priests in the Temple. Mary and Joseph
searched for him for three days. When they finally found him,
Jesus said to them, "I have to be in my Father's house."

The scribes and priests

A scroll of the Scriptures

Mary and Joseph find Jesus.

The Jerusalem Temple

The Baptism of Jesus

When Jesus was thirty, he was baptized by John the Baptist.
The Holy Spirit came down upon him like a dove.
From the heavens, God said, "Here is my beloved Son,
whom I have chosen."

"Change your hearts," says John the Baptist.

The water   Baptism   The dove

"This is the Lamb of God," says John the Baptist.

The Call of the Apostles

"Come and follow me!" said Jesus. Peter and his brother Andrew followed him, and then James and his brother John. They were joined by Philip, Bartholomew, Thomas, Matthew, James the son of Alphaeus, Thaddaeus (or Jude), Simon, and Judas.

A boat

Fishermen

A net

Fish

The call of Jesus

The Twelve Apostles

Jesus Is the Word of God

Jesus proclaimed the Good News to everyone, to little ones and grown-ups: "God is our Father. He loves you and forgives you. He invites you to live for ever in his kingdom of love."

The people

A beggar

A cripple

The Good News is proclaimed to all.

Thank you, Lord!

God loves us.

He is our Father.

Like a Grain of Wheat

Jesus said, "When a grain of wheat falls among the rocks or thorns, it cannot grow. But when it is planted in good soil, it grows and bears fruit. In the same way, the Word of God bears fruit when it is welcomed within a good heart."

The sower

A grain of wheat

Good soil

Thorns

Birds

Rocks

An ear of wheat

The reaper

Bread

The Good Shepherd

The shepherd and his sheep

The lost sheep

The sheep is found.

The shepherd's joy

Jesus said, "When a sheep is lost, the good shepherd goes out looking for it. When he finds it, he brings it back with great joy. Your Father in heaven, too, always goes out searching for anyone who goes astray."

The Vine Grower and His Vine

The vine grower

The vine and its branches

Grapes

The winepress

Wine

Jesus said, "My Father is the vine grower.
I am the vine, and you are the branches. Remain in me,
and I will make you fruitful."

The Miracles of Jesus

5 loaves of bread and 2 fish

Jesus multiplies the loaves.

5,000 people eat their fill.

Jesus performed miracles to show
that the love of God is all-powerful.

At Cana, Jesus turns water into wine.

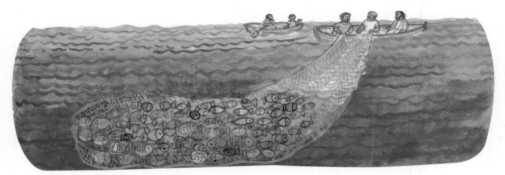

Thanks to Jesus, there is a huge catch of fish.

Jesus calms a storm at sea.

Jesus Forgives and Heals

The paralyzed man walks.

Zacchaeus has
a change of heart.

Blind Bartimaeus sees.

The leper is healed.

Jesus changed hearts. In the name of God, he forgave
and healed. To those who believe in him, he gives life.

The Samaritan woman
accepts the Savior.

The deaf-mute hears
and speaks.

The daughter of Jairus
comes back to life.

The children are blessed.

Palm Sunday

Jesus entered Jerusalem. The crowds waved palm branches.
"Hosanna! Blessed be Jesus. He is our king!"
They laid their cloaks down like a carpet under
the hooves of his little gray donkey.

Jesus' entrance into Jerusalem

Palm branches

Hosanna!

The cloaks

The disciples

Jesus the King

The crowd

79

Jesus' Last Supper

The washing of the feet

Jesus' Last Supper with his Apostles

Jesus said to his Apostles, "Love each other as I have loved you." He gave them Communion, saying, "Do this in memory of me."

This is my Body.

This is my Blood.

The Bread of life

The Chalice of salvation

The first Communion

Judas' betrayal

On the Mount of Olives

During the night, Jesus prayed. His Apostles fell asleep.
Judas had betrayed him, but Jesus offered up his life:
"Father, may your will be done."

An olive tree

The prayer of Jesus

The sleeping
Apostles

Jesus' arrest

The kiss of Judas

The prisoner Jesus

30 pieces of silver

The Way of the Cross

Jesus was beaten and crowned with thorns. He was made
to carry a heavy cross. Then soldiers crucified him. Jesus,
who had never done any wrong, forgave everyone
and offered his life for the love of us all.

The cross

The crown
of thorns

Soldiers

The crucifixion

Jesus dies on the cross.

The burial in the tomb

The closed tomb

Easter Morning

On Easter Sunday, early in the morning,
women came with perfumed oils. But Jesus was no longer
in the tomb. The angel of the Lord said to them, "Jesus is risen.
He is alive for ever!" Alleluia!

Peter and John

The open tomb

The shroud

Jesus appears to Mary Magdalene.

Perfumed oils

The angel
of the Lord

Alleluia!

The Risen Jesus

"Peace be with you," said Jesus to his joyous disciples.
"Go out into the world and tell everyone about the love of God!"

On the road to Emmaus

The breaking of bread

The risen Jesus on the lakeshore

At the Ascension, Jesus returns to his Father.

Pentecost

The Apostles had gathered together to pray with Mary.
Suddenly, a great wind blew through the house, and tongues
of fire came down upon each of them. They were filled
with the Holy Spirit.

The wind of the Holy Spirit

The tongues of fire

The Apostles tell everyone about the Good News.

They baptize in the name of the Father, and of the Son, and of the Holy Spirit.

The First Christians

The teaching of the Apostles

Sharing

Praise and thanksgiving

The breaking of bread

"I am with you for ever," said Jesus. The Word of God was shared, and the number of Christians grew. Through the strength of the Holy Spirit, they spread the Gospel throughout the earth.

Stephen the martyr

Paul's conversion

Peter, the head
of the Church

The voyages of Paul

The letters of Paul

The Church gathers together through the Holy Spirit.

Under the direction of Romain Lizé, Vice President, Magnificat
Editor, Magnificat: Isabelle Galmiche
Editor, Ignatius: Vivian Dudro
Translator: Janet Chevrier
Proofreader: Claire Gilligan
Assistant to the Editor: Pascale van de Walle
Layout Designers: Elisabeth Hebert, Gauthier Delauné, Le Semeur d'Images
Production: Thierry Dubus, Sabine Marioni

Original French edition: *Mon Imagier de la Bible*
© 2012 by Mame, Paris.
© 2017 by Magnificat, New York • Ignatius Press, San Francisco

Printed in June 2017 by TWP, Malaysia
Job number MGN17014
Printed in compliance with the Consumer Protection Safety Act, 2008.